*For my mother, who taught
me to love the Book of Mormon*

—TR

For Holly

—JM

Text © 2001 Timothy M. Robinson
Illustrations © 2001 James Allen Madsen

Bookcraft is a registered trademark of Deseret Book Company.

Visit us at www.deseretbook.com

Library of Congress Card Number: 2001086371

ISBN 1-57345-840-6

Printed in the United States of America   42316-6736

10   9   8   7   6   5   4   3   2   1

A FOUNTAIN OF PURE WATER

A Nephite Baptism Story

Written by Timothy Robinson
Illustrated by Jim Madsen

BOOKCRAFT

SALT LAKE CITY, UTAH

They've taken him and bound him."

"He will surely be put to death!"

There was muttering all through the streets. And I knew they were speaking of Abinadi, the prophet who had returned to preach against the king. I had seen him standing on boxes in the market square, his eyes like fire.

He spoke of Jesus and said we should repent. But the people were angry at his words and took him to the palace.

MOSIAH 12:1–3, 9

Later in the week, when Sarah and I were playing by the road, she shouted, "Look!" And I looked up to see one of the royal priests riding toward us. His heavy robes were flapping behind him and his horse's feet were a blur.

"The king has called his counselors," Mother explained when we told her what we had seen. "I've heard it in the streets. That man will help Noah decide what to do with the prophet." MOSIAH 12:17

Ever since King Zeniff died, the streets were filled with whispers and rumors. With Zeniff, the people felt safe. But now his son King Noah ruled, and there were secrets.

Father was a royal tax collector, which used to bring our family honor. Now he was feared and hated. King Noah sent him far and wide collecting gold and silver, animals and grain to pay for the King's many wives and priests. MOSIAH 11:1–4

When Father came home that night, his face was pale with worry. "They're going to burn him," he said to Mother. "When I delivered my collections, the soldiers told me so."

I did not mean to overhear, but now I too was filled with worry. "Who, Father, who?" I asked.

"Oh, little one," he said, turning to see me. "Abinadi, the prophet. But perhaps all will still be well. One of the king's own priests is pleading for the prophet's life." MOSIAH 17:1–2

But Alma, the priest, was soon banished from the court. The king sent his servants to find him and kill him, if they could. And when Mother, Sarah, and I went to do the wash, one of the women at the river claimed he was already dead.

Another said no, that he was still alive and was preaching God's word. Mother asked where, and the woman said in the forest—deep in the forest where foolish boys went to hunt wild beasts for fur. MOSIAH 17:3, 18:1–4

Next morning, Mother woke me early, before the sun, and urged me to gather up food for our journey. "Journey?" I asked. "Where are we going?"

"Hunting," she said, and I knew then that we would look for Alma.

Father had to stay behind. It would not do for him to be missed at the palace. There were harsh penalties for tax collectors who collected nothing.

Sarah stayed with a friend. Her feet were too little for the road.

We walked all morning and into the afternoon. My legs were heavy when we finally stopped to rest near a land called Mormon. As I sat down and pulled bread from my sack, I thought I heard a voice. The sound came again and I was sure. It was voices, many voices, not far from where we were.

We pushed through the trees and bushes until we came to a clearing by a lake. MOSIAH 18:5–6

There were people by the lake, hundreds of them. And standing in the middle of them was a man with bright eyes. He was talking and moving his hands. And the words he spoke were the words of Christ—how we should comfort sad people and stand as witnesses of God. They were Abinadi's words, and my heart seemed to jump when I heard them. MOSIAH 18:7–9

Behold," he said, "here are the waters of Mormon . . . and now, as ye are desirous to come into the fold of God, and to be called his people, . . . what have you against being baptized in the name of the Lord?"

When he finished speaking, the crowd clapped their hands and cheered. Many pressed forward. I stepped forward too, but Mother reached out and held me back.

MOSIAH 18:8, 10–11

No," she said, "not without your father. We must go and tell what we have seen. We must bring him too." So we turned and walked away from that beautiful place. And the journey home seemed a hundred miles. MOSIAH 18:30

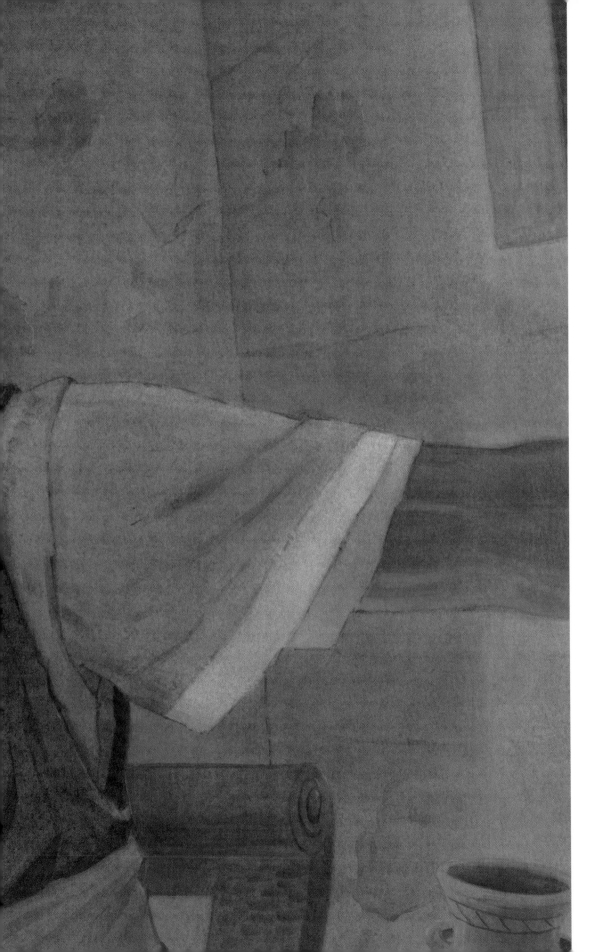

Later that night, when I was so exhausted I should have been sleeping, I lay awake, restless, listening to Mother and Father whispering by the fire, watching Sarah toss and turn with her dreams.

I must have finally slept, for suddenly, it seemed, the sun was up.

"Little one," I heard. It was Father. "I will not go to the king today," he told me.

My eyes grew round with fear. "Father, they will come for you!"

"And I will not be here. We are going to the forest. Today." He said it as though it were a grave and terrible thing. "We are going to see Alma, the new prophet, for Abinadi has been killed."

MOSIAH 17:13–15, 20

We packed, but only what we could carry: food, clothing, and Father let me take my doll. Mother wrapped Sarah with cloth and tied her to Father's back. We would not return home again.

I started crying, though I didn't know why. I tried to think about Alma and the beautiful words. I tried to think about the clear blue lake.

We walked and walked and the sun pushed down on the bundle on my back. Sarah whimpered in the heat.

Later, as if in a dream, we came to the place where we had first heard the voices. Suddenly there were people all around us, lifting the bundles off our backs.

And then, at a distance, I saw Alma. He made his way toward us, his bright eyes smiling. He welcomed us. He asked if we believed in Christ. And when Father told our story, Alma led us to the lake, a fountain of pure water hidden by the trees.

MOSIAH 18:5

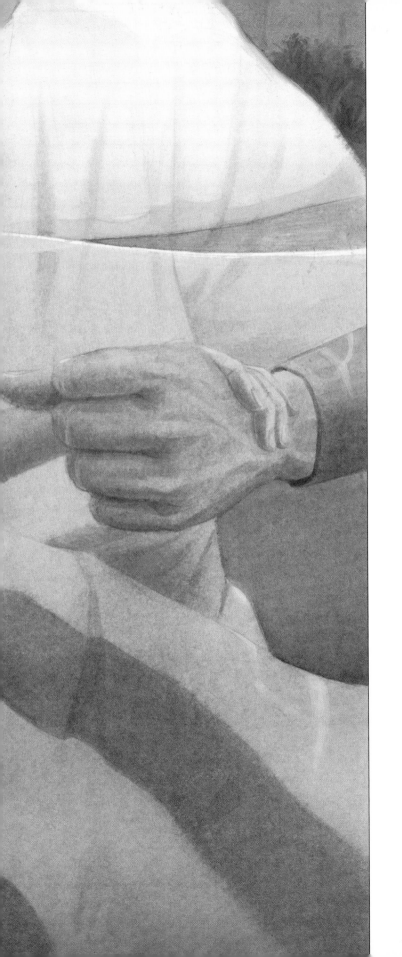

Alma baptized Father, then Mother, and then it was my turn—Sarah was still too young.

I waded into the water, cool against my skin. Alma held my wrist with one hand and raised his other hand to the sky. He spoke beautiful words about having authority from God. I felt the water cover my face and body and for a moment all was quiet.

Then I was out in the breeze again. I turned and smiled at Father and Mother and little Sarah. I felt the peace in my heart.

MOSIAH 18:12–13, 16–17

EPILOGUE

Alma's little band of faithful Saints suffered much before their wanderings in the wilderness were through. Soon King Noah's spies found them and soldiers came. Alma and his people ran away to the land of Helam, where they were captured by the Lamanites. Forced into slavery and threatened with death if they called out to God, Alma's people prayed silently in their hearts for comfort. When they were baptized, they had covenanted to "bear one another's burdens, that they may be light" (Mosiah 18:8). A burden is something that is heavy to carry. As slaves, Alma's people were forced to carry heavy things such as rocks and dirt, but the Lord himself "did strengthen them that they could bear up their burdens with ease" (Mosiah 24:15), even that they "[could] not feel them upon [their] backs" (Mosiah 24:14).

Today, when we are baptized into The Church of Jesus Christ of Latter-day Saints, we too covenant to "mourn with those that mourn," and "comfort those that stand in need of comfort" (Mosiah 18:9). We witness to our Heavenly Father that we will "serve him and keep his commandments" (Mosiah 18:10). And just like the little girl in this story, we leave behind our old life and embrace a new one among "his people" (Mosiah 18:8). When we do this we are promised that he will "pour out his Spirit more abundantly" upon us (Mosiah 18:10).

We, too, can feel peace in our hearts when we are baptized.